# WILL SHAKESPEARE SAVE US!
# WILL SHAKESPEARE SAVE THE KING!

Two one act plays

## PAUL NIMMO

DRAMATIC LINES, TWICKENHAM, ENGLAND
text copyright © Paul Nimmo

Dramatic Lines
PO Box 201
Twickenham
TW2 5RQ
England

A CIP record for this book is
available from the British Library

ISBN 0 9522224 1 8

Will Shakespeare Save Us!
Will Shakespeare Save the King!
first published 1995 by
Dramatic Lines
Twickenham England
reprinted 2001

Printed by The Dramatic Lines Press
Twickenham England

*'Chunks of Shakespeare wrapped up in a bit of fun'*

Paul Nimmo

---

I wrote both plays because I was asked to by the Young Friends of Shakespeare's Globe at Giggleswick School (my old school). They wanted to present some of the Best Bits of the Bard to other schools without having to grind through all thirty-seven plays in one double period. So here are some of the most famous scenes and speeches from *Hamlet, Romeo and Juliet, Julius Caesar, A Midsummer Night's Dream, The Tempest, Henry V, As You Like It, Twelfth Night, Much Ado About Nothing, Richard III* and *Henry IV part 1*.

I've enjoyed reading, watching and performing in Shakespeare's plays ever since my English teacher cast me as Falstaff when I was eleven. The plays are old, the language is often difficult and some of the jokes are just... well! I think you had to be there. But they're still worth bothering with – the plays, not the jokes. If you look hard you can see they're about people like you, your friends, your family and how they all fit together. OK, you might not be at war with the French, sword-fighting in Italy or murdering a king in the highlands of Scotland but you will feel, sooner or later, the love, hate, fear, courage, betrayal, complete humiliation and utter triumph that Shakespeare's plays are about.

And you can get all this just from being in one of them!

The Playwright would like to thank Jonathan Broadbent for inspiring him to write these plays and Michael Day for inspiring him to write.

# USING THE PLAYS

The plays are suitable for the 11-18 year age range and have been successfully produced with actors of varying ages within the same cast.

You can use the scripts in a variety of ways. WILL SHAKESPEARE SAVE THE KING! works as a sequel to WILL SHAKESPEARE SAVE US! so you can present both as The School Play in a double bill (doing both would mean that everyone in the cast could take at least one major Shakespearean role). Alternatively you can present either play on its own, perhaps the first one term and the second one the following term, using the same cast. When considering your audience bear in mind that these plays appeal to all ages and have been successfully performed on tour; many people who wouldn't go to see a Shakespeare play performed have been surprised and delighted.

The scripts are ideal for reading aloud by classes or groups. It's probably best to try and have everyone read at least a few lines of Shakespeare, but it's equally important to remember that the scenes were written for performance, so do get your readers standing up, moving around and stabbing each other to death... where the script calls for it. Also, have people swapping roles and always encourage the others to suggest how a scene might be staged or a line delivered.

You can concentrate more fully on the 'chunks of Shakespeare', though don't forget that the framework story is a genuinely enjoyable route into those speeches and scenes and a way of exploring more Shakespeare than the year's set text.

Whatever you do, have fun!

# PRODUCTION REQUIREMENTS

## Cast

*Minimum cast is ten* – three principals plus seven Players for either play.

Both plays have the same principal characters: King (or Queen), Chamberlain and Director. They have parts specifically written for eight Players but you can always have more and re-allocate the lines. The minimum number of Players for either play is seven to present the scene from *A Midsummer Night's Dream* in **WILL SHAKESPEARE SAVE US!** and the scene from *Henry IV part 1* in **WILL SHAKESPEARE SAVE THE KING!**

## Set

There are no specific set requirements for either play apart from a throne for the King. You could create a chamber in the King's castle but the more flexible you leave your acting space the better as each play contains such a variety of scenes.

You may find it useful to have different levels for presenting the various scenes (benches and large hamper-style baskets have proved effective in previous productions) as well as an area which is clearly 'offstage' i.e. a place from which the principals and the other Players can watch.

## Props

These are the props you must have for each play any others are up to you.

### WILL SHAKESPEARE SAVE US!

An old 'Shakespeare' volume, dog, bush, lantern, fake sword, crown, taper/candle, two swords/foils, goblet.
Lion's head/mask, 'Wall', bloodstained cloak. *(A Midsummer Night's Dream)*

### WILL SHAKESPEARE SAVE THE KING!

An old 'Shakespeare' volume, goblet, poison bottle, foil, birthday cake.
Falstaff padding/cushion *(Henry IV, part 1)*

## Costumes

For either play, you need at the very least, similar costumes for all the Players, a crown and cloak for the King and a cloak for the Chamberlain. As the setting is basically fairy-tale you can add variety and richness to your production with the costumes worn by the Players in the Shakespearean scenes (but note that there isn't much time for changing).

An alternative to costume is for the cast to dress in black.

WILL SHAKESPEARE
SAVE US!

# WILL SHAKESPEARE SAVE US!

*(The King sits slumped on his raised throne: looks very, very bored. Drums fingers. Sighs. Enter Lord Chamberlain)*

**CHAMBERLAIN**  *(Bowing)* Sire, you sent for me.

**KING**  Yes, Lord Chamberlain.

**CHAMBERLAIN**  What is your majesty's pleasure?

**KING**  I'm bored.

**CHAMBERLAIN**  Sire?

**KING**  Bored, you oaf, bored! Bored, bored, bored, bored, BORED!

**CHAMBERLAIN**  I see. Can I interest you majesty in... a game of Scrabble?

**KING**  No.

**CHAMBERLAIN**  Would the royal stomach enjoy a sumptuous banquet?

**KING**  No.

**CHAMBERLAIN**  Cup of tea?

**KING**  No! I'm *bored*, Lord Chamberlain, bored! Fed up to the back teeth, uninterested, unamused, uninspired and most of all BORED!

*(The Lord Chamberlain is almost blown over by this last outburst)*

**KING**  Where are the players?

**CHAMBERLAIN**  Sire, I will summon them at once.

**KING**  Good. Tell them I'm bored. Tell them they'd better amuse me – or else. Understood?

**CHAMBERLAIN**  Perfectly.

*(Exit Lord Chamberlain. The King goes on being bored. Lord Chamberlain returns)*

**CHAMBERLAIN**  *(Triumphantly)* Your majesty – the players!

*(Enter the players, in a shambles. They form up and do a pathetic Morris dance very badly to a simple musical accompaniment. The Lord Chamberlain claps merrily to no particular rhythm. The King stares in disbelief)*

**KING**  *(Low)* Stop it. *(Rising)* Stop it. *(Bellowing)* STOP IT!

*(The players stop in their tracks and gape at him)*

1

| | |
|---|---|
| **KING** | Now listen, you pathetic lot. |
| | *(He steps down from his throne and walks amongst them)* |
| **KING** | I... am... *(In a player's ear)* BORED! And if you players can't come up with something better than this to entertain me, then here's what I'm going to do. I'm going to liven up my day by having each and every one of you tortured *(They wince)*, hung, drawn and quartered *(Gasp)* and then slowly disembowelled *(Groan)*.<br>Now, I don't like violence – but I'm so *(In another ear)* BORED that if you can't entertain me when you're living, you may as well do it when you're dying – all right? Good. Be back here with something interesting by noon tomorrow, and remember – your lives depend on it! |
| | *(Exit King)* |
| **CHAMBERLAIN** | *(Manic)* Right! You heard him. Noon tomorrow – and your lives depend on it! |
| **DIRECTOR** | But Lord Chamberlain, we... |
| **CHAMBERLAIN** | *(Shrieking)* Silence! I don't want to know! |
| | *(Exit Lord Chamberlain)* |
| **PLAYER 1** | Oh my God, we're all going to die! |
| **PLAYER 2** | You're right – we don't stand a chance. |
| **DIRECTOR** | Shut up, shut up! That's quite enough of that! I have absolutely no intention of dying, so we're all going to pull together and give the King the show of his life. Now, has anyone got any ideas? |
| **PLAYER 1** | We may as well just stab ourselves in front of him. |
| **PLAYER 2** | Yeah – cut out the middle man. |
| **DIRECTOR** | Quiet! |
| **PLAYER 3** | We could do a pantomime. |
| **DIRECTOR** | Hmmm. |
| **PLAYER 4** | Or circus acts. |
| **DIRECTOR** | Hmmm. |
| **PLAYER 5** | Or a musical. |
| **DIRECTOR** | No. The King is bored. We have to present something which will engage his imagination, make him think, stir up his emotions. |

| | |
|---|---|
| **DIRECTOR** | We need something with sex, violence, political intrigue, madness, comedy and most important of all – a good part for me. |
| **PLAYER 6** | How about Shakespeare? |
| **DIRECTOR** | Who? |
| **PLAYER 6** | William Shakespeare. |
| **DIRECTOR** | Who on earth is he? |
| **PLAYER 7** | Some old English playwright. |
| **DIRECTOR** | Some old English playwright, is he! Will Shakespeare save our lives? |
| **PLAYER 6** | Yes – because he's got everything you said. |
| **PLAYER 8** | Yes – and more. |
| **DIRECTOR** | Prove it. |
| **PLAYER 6** | All right. See this book? It's called Famous Speeches from Shakespeare. I found it in the Royal Library. There's some terrific stuff in here – we could all do a bit. Listen, I've learnt the first one; I was going to use it as an audition piece. |
| **PLAYER 4** | You didn't tell us you were going for an audition. |
| **PLAYER 6** | No, I... |
| **PLAYER 5** | Stab you in the back, he would, soon as look at you. |
| **PLAYER 6** | Look... |
| **PLAYER 1** | He won't need to if we don't get a move on – the King's guards'll do it for him. |
| **DIRECTOR** | Enough! Now, give us your speech. It may be our only chance. |
| **PLAYER 6** | Right.<br>O! for a mu... |
| **DIRECTOR** | *(Interrupting)* When you're ready. |
| **PLAYER 6** | Yes – I *am* ready. |
| **DIRECTOR** | Good. Well get on with it then. |

**PLAYER 6**     O for a mu...

Oh hang on – I'd better tell you a bit about it. It introduces Shakespeare's play *Henry V*, which is full of battles. The playwright is asking the people in the audience to use their imaginations, because you can't really show a full-scale medieval battle in a theatre. So the actors have to pretend – and so does the audience.

*[Prologue to Henry V]*

O for a muse of fire, that would ascend
The brightest heaven of invention:
A kingdom for a stage, princes to act,
And monarchs to behold the swelling scene!
Then should the warlike Harry, like himself,
Assume the port of Mars, and at his heels
(Leashed in, like hounds) should famine, sword and fire
Crouch for employment. But pardon, gentles all,
The flat unraiséd spirits that hath dared
On this unworthy scaffold to bring forth
So great an object. Can this cockpit hold
The vasty fields of France? Or may we cram
Within this wooden O the very casques
That did affright the air at Agincourt?
O, pardon – since a crooked figure may
Attest in little place a million;
And let us, ciphers to this great account,
On your imaginary forces work.
Suppose within the girdle of these walls
Are now confined two mighty monarchies.
Whose high, uprearéd and abutting fronts
The perilous narrow ocean parts asunder.
Piece out our imperfections with your thoughts:
Into a thousand parts divide one man
And make imaginary puissance.
Think, when we talk of horses, that you see them
Printing their proud hoofs i' th' receiving earth;
For 'tis your thoughts that now must deck our kings.
Turning th' accomplishment of many years
Into an hourglass; for the which supply,
Admit me, Chorus to this history;
Who, Prologue-like, your humble patience pray,
Gently to hear, kindly to judge our play.

**DIRECTOR**     *(After a pause)* Hmm. Not bad.

**PLAYER 2**     Not bad, it was absolutely brilliant!

| | |
|---|---|
| **PLAYER 1** | Are there more speeches like that? |
| **PLAYER 8** | Yeah, loads. |
| **PLAYER 3** | We could all do one. |
| **PLAYER 4** | What, together? |
| **PLAYER 5** | No, one each. |
| **DIRECTOR** | Please! I believe I am the director here, so I will make the decisions. We will all look in the book, choose a speech, learn it in the next hour and come back and perform it. If the general standard is as high as we've just seen, we'll perform this Shakespeare to the King. If not, you can start deciding who's going to be the back end of Daisy the pantomime cow. |
| | *(All freeze. Time is seen, or heard, to pass.*<br>*All gather round the Director.*<br>*The following brief performances are all terribly mannered and over-acted)* |
| **DIRECTOR** | All right – so what have we got? |
| **PLAYER 1** | *(Standing)* To be... |
| **DIRECTOR** | Hang on, hang on – what play is this from, what's going on? |
| **PLAYER 1** | It's from something called *Hamlet;* it's when the hero considers the meaning of life and death. |
| **DIRECTOR** | Something light then. Well, get on with it. |
| **PLAYER 1** | To be or not to be, that is the question,<br>Whether 'tis... |
| **DIRECTOR** | Next! |
| **PLAYER 2** | This is the opening of *Richard III.*<br>Now is the winter of our discontent<br>Made glorious summer by this sun of York;<br>And... |
| **DIRECTOR** | Next! |
| **PLAYER 3** | This is Macbeth, seeing things.<br>Is this a dagger that I see before me? |
| **DIRECTOR** | Next! |
| **PLAYER 4** | Juliet talks of her lover Romeo.<br>Oh, Romeo, Romeo – wherefore art thou Romeo? |
| **DIRECTOR** | Next! |

| **PLAYER 5** | Portia describes mercy in *The Merchant of Venice*. |
| | The quality of mercy is not strained, |
| | It droppeth... |
| **DIRECTOR** | Next! |
| **PLAYER 7** | Orsino opens *Twelfth Night*. |
| | If music be the food of love, play on... |
| **DIRECTOR** | Get off! This is hopeless! You're useless, the lot of you. That *Henry V* speech was good because... because... well, why was it good? |
| **PLAYER 8** | Because he said it naturally, as if it was him talking in his usual way – not as if he was an actor, hamming it up. |
| **DIRECTOR** | Yes, that's right. |
| **PLAYER 8** | I've got one. It's Mark Antony's speech over the body of Julius Caesar, who's just been stabbed by the senators of Rome. Mark Antony mourns for his friend – but he also plans revenge... |
| **DIRECTOR** | Right – let's hear it then. |

[*Julius Caesar* III,i]

O, pardon me, thou bleeding piece of earth,
That I am meek and gentle with these butchers!
Thou art the ruins of the noblest man
That ever lived in the tide of times.
Woe to the hand that shed this costly blood!
Over thy wounds now do I prophesy,
Which like dumb mouths do ope their ruby lips
To be the voice and utterance of my tongue,
A curse shall light upon the limbs of men;
Domestic fury and fierce civil strife
Shall cumber all the parts of Italy;
Blood and destruction shall be so in use,
And dreadful objects so familiar,
That mothers shall but smile when they behold
Their infants quartered with the hands of war;
All pity choked with custom of fell deeds:
And Caesar's spirit, ranging for revenge,
With Ate by his side come hot from hell,
Still in these confines with a monarch's voice
Cry "Havoc", and let slip the dogs of war;
That this foul deed shall smell above the earth
With carrion men, groaning for burial.

(Stunned silence)

6

| | |
|---|---|
| **DIRECTOR** | Hmm. Pretty good. |
| **PLAYER 2** | Pretty good – that was stunning! |
| **DIRECTOR** | Yes, there may be some hope after all. |
| **PLAYER 6** | No – we need to do scenes from Shakespeare – have more than one actor on at a time. |
| **DIRECTOR** | What? |
| **PLAYER 6** | We need dialogue, interaction, drama, conflict – the King might get fed up just listening to one of us. |
| **DIRECTOR** | Damnit, you're right. |
| **PLAYER 1** | *(Sarcastically)* Why not do Shakespeare's Complete Works, then? We've got all of twenty hours to rehearse them. |
| **DIRECTOR** | No, scenes it must be – and we need to present a variety. Does the book have scenes from Shakespeare in it? |
| **PLAYER 7** | No. |
| **PLAYER 5** | Only speeches. |
| **PLAYER 6** | There's bound to be more Shakespeare in the Royal Library. |
| **DIRECTOR** | Yes, right, come on you lot – let's go and find Shakespeare. |
| | *(Exit all. Enter King. He sits on his throne, wild-eyed with boredom. Enter Lord Chamberlain, in a hurry)* |
| **CHAMBERLAIN** | Your majesty, they're ready. |
| **KING** | *(Vaguely)* What? |
| **CHAMBERLAIN** | The players, sire – they're ready to perform for you. You told them to be here at noon. |
| **KING** | *(Dreamily)* Noon? *(Waking up)* Oh yes – so I did.*(With glee)* I was going to have them tortured, wasn't I. |
| **CHAMBERLAIN** | *(Delicately)* Only if you weren't entertained by their presentation, your majesty. |
| **KING** | What? Oh yes, yes – but it's bound to be awful, isn't it. All right, send 'em in. |
| | *(Lord Chamberlain ushers in the players. They enter in orderly fashion, form a line and bow in unison to the King)* |
| **DIRECTOR** | *(Stepping forward)* Your majesty, we present some scenes from the plays of William Shakespeare. |

| | |
|---|---|
| **KING** | *(To Lord Chamberlain)* Who? |
| **CHAMBERLAIN** | William Shakespeare, my lord. |
| **KING** | Yes I heard that, you dolt – who is he? Do I know him? |
| **CHAMBERLAIN** | Hardly, sire. He's been dead for centuries. |
| **KING** | Lucky for him. |
| **DIRECTOR** | *(Getting on with it)* Sire, our first scene is a short one... |
| **KING** | Good. |
| **DIRECTOR** | ...from Romeo and Juliet. The story is of a boy and girl who fall in love in spite of the fact that their families hate each other. This is the moment when they first meet; they're so inspired by each other that they use the language of religion.<br><br>[*Romeo and Juliet* I,v] |
| **ROMEO** | *(Taking Juliet's hand)* If I profane with my unworthiest hand<br>This holy shrine, the gentle sin is this:<br>My lips, two blushing pilgrims, ready stand<br>To smooth that rough touch with a tender kiss. |
| **JULIET** | Good pilgrim, you do wrong your hand too much,<br>Which mannerly devotion shows in this;<br>For saints have hands that pilgrims' hands do touch,<br>And palm to palm is holy palmer's kiss. |
| **ROMEO** | Have not saints lips, and holy palmers too? |
| **JULIET** | Ay, pilgrim, lips that they must use in prayer. |
| **ROMEO** | O then, dear saint, let lips do what hands do:<br>They pray – grant thou, lest faith turn to despair. |
| **JULIET** | Saints do not move, though grant for prayers' sake. |
| **ROMEO** | Then move not, while my prayers' effect I take.<br><br>*(They kiss)* |
| **ROMEO** | Thus from my lips, by thine, my sin is purged. |
| **JULIET** | Then have my lips the sin that they have took. |

| ROMEO | Sin from my lips? Oh trespass sweetly urged! Give me my sin again. |
|---|---|
| | *(They kiss)* |
| JULIET | You kiss by the book! |
| | *(The actors face the King and bow before returning to the group)* |
| CHAMBERLAIN | I'm so sorry, your majesty – shall I call the torturers? |
| KING | Hang on, hang on, Lord Chamberlain. That wasn't too bad. |
| CHAMBERLAIN | *(Amazed)* Sire? |
| KING | Well I can't say I understood a word of it, but you could tell they believed it – love at first sight and all that. |
| CHAMBERLAIN | Er, yes... of course, sire. |
| KING | Never been in love, Lord Chamberlain? |
| CHAMBERLAIN | Well... |
| KING | *(Nostalgically)* I remember when I was in love... |
| DIRECTOR | *(Tentatively)* Your majesty. |
| KING | What? Oh yes – well, get on with it then. I'm still bored, you know. |
| DIRECTOR | Yes, your majesty. We now present a whole play within a play. It's the story of Pyramus and Thisbe, as performed for Theseus by the Rude Mechanicals in *A Midsummer Night's Dream*. |
| | *[Midsummer Night's Dream V,i]* |
| QUINCE | If we offend it is with our good will. That you should think we come not to offend But with good will. To show our simple skill, That is the true beginning of our end. Consider then we come but in despite. We do not come as minding to content you, Our true intent is. All for your delight We are not here. That you should here repent you The actors are at hand, and by their show You shall know all that you are like to know. |
| | *(Enter Bottom as Pyramus, Flute as Thisbe, Snout as Wall, Starveling as Moonshine and Snug as Lion)* |

**QUINCE**　Gentles, perchance you wonder at this show;
But wonder on, till truth make all things plain.
This man is Pyramus, if you would know;
This beauteous lady Thisbe is, certain.
This man with lime and roughcast doth present
Wall – that vile wall which did these lovers sunder;
And through Wall's chink, poor souls, they are content
To whisper. At the which let no man wonder.
This man with lantern, dog and bush of thorn
Presenteth Moonshine. For if you will know
By moonshine did these lovers think no scorn
To meet at Ninus' tomb, there, there to woo.
This grisly beast – which Lion hight by name –
The trusty Thisbe coming first by night
Did scare away, or rather did affright.
And as she fled, her mantle did she fall,
Which Lion vile with bloody mouth did stain.
Anon comes Pyramus – sweet youth and tall –
And finds his trusty Thisbe's mantle slain.
Whereat with blade – with bloody, blameful blade –
He bravely broached his boiling bloody breast.
And Thisbe, tarrying in mulberry shade,
His dagger drew, and died. For all the rest,
Let Lion, Moonshine, Wall and lovers twain
At large discourse while here they do remain.

*(Exit Quince, Bottom, Flute, Snug and Starveling)*

**SNOUT/WALL**　In this same interlude it doth befall
That I – one Snout by name – present a wall.
And such a wall as I would have you think
That had in it a crannied hole or chink,
Through which the lovers, Pyramus and Thisbe,
Did whisper often, very secretly.
This loam, this roughcast, and this stone doth show
That I am that same wall; the truth is so.

*(Snout holds out fingers)*

**SNOUT/WALL**　And this the cranny is, right and sinister,
Through which the fearful lovers are to whisper.

*(Enter Bottom as Pyramus)*

**BOTT/PYRAMUS**　O grim-looked night, O night with hue so black,
O night which ever art when day is not!
O night, O night, alack, alack, alack,
I fear my Thisbe's promise is forgot.

| BOTT/PYRAMUS | And thou, O Wall, O sweet, O lovely Wall,<br>That standest between her father's ground and mine,<br>Thou Wall, O Wall, O sweet, O lovely Wall,<br>Show me thy chink to blink through with mine eyne. |
|---|---|

*(Snout holds out fingers)*

| BOTT/PYRAMUS | Thanks, courteous Wall; Jove shield thee well for this.<br>But what see I? No Thisbe do I see.<br>O wicked Wall, through whom I see no bliss:<br>Cursed be thy stones for thus deceiving me! |
|---|---|
| THESEUS | The Wall, methinks, being sensible, should curse again. |
| BOTTOM | No, in truth sir, he should not. "Deceiving me" is Thisbe's cue. She is to enter now, and I am to spy her through the wall. You shall see – it will fall pat as I told you. Yonder she comes. |

*(Enter Flute as Thisbe)*

| FLUTE/THISBE | O Wall, full often hast thou heard my moans<br>For parting my fair Pyramus and me.<br>My cherry lips have often kissed thy stones,<br>Thy stones with lime and hair knit up in thee. |
|---|---|
| BOTT/PYRAMUS | I see a voice. Now will I to the chink<br>To spy an I can hear my Thisbe's face.<br>Thisbe! |
| FLUTE/THISBE | My love! Thou art my love, I think? |
| BOTT/PYRAMUS | Think what thou wilt, I am thy lover's grace,<br>And like Limander am I trusty still. |
| FLUTE/THISBE | And I like Helen till the Fates me kill. |
| BOTT/PYRAMUS | Not Shafalus to Procrus was so true. |
| FLUTE/THISBE | As Shafalus to Procrus, I to you. |
| BOTT/PYRAMUS | O, kiss me through the hole of this vile Wall! |
| FLUTE/THISBE | I kiss the Wall's hole, not your lips at all. |
| BOTT/PYRAMUS | Wilt thou at Ninny's tomb meet me straight way? |
| FLUTE/THISBE | Tide life, tide death, I come without delay. |

*(Exit Bottom and Flute)*

| SNOUT/WALL | Thus have I, Wall, my part dischargéd so; |
|---|---|
| | And being done, thus Wall away doth go. |

*(Exit Snout. Enter Snug as Lion and Starveling as Moonshine)*

**SNUG/LION**

You, ladies – you whose gentle hearts do fear
The smallest monstrous mouse that creeps on floor –
May now, perchance, both quake and tremble here,
When Lion rough in wildest rage doth roar.
Then know that I as Snug the joiner am
A lion fell, nor else no lion's dam,
For if I should as Lion come in strife
Into this place, 'twere pity on my life.

**STARVE/MOON**

This lanthorn doth the hornéd moon present;
Myself the man i' th' moon do seem to be.
All I have to say is to tell you that the lantern is the moon,
I the man i' th' moon, this thorn bush my thorn bush,
and this dog my dog.

*(Enter Flute as Thisbe)*

**FLUTE/THISBE**

This is old Ninny's tomb. Where is my love?

*(Snug roars. Flute runs off. Snug tears Thisbe's mantle.
Exit Snug. Enter Bottom)*

**BOTT/PYRAMUS**

Sweet moon, I thank thee for thy sunny beams;
I thank thee, moon, for shining now so bright;
For by thy gracious, golden, glittering beams
I trust to take of truest Thisbe sight.
But stay – O spite!
But mark, poor Knight,
What dreadful dole is here?
Eyes, do you see?
How can it be?
O dainty duck, O dear!
Thy mantle good –
What, stained with blood!
Approach, ye Furies fell.
O Fates, come, come,
Cut thread and thrum,
Quail, crush, conclude and quell.
O wherefore, Nature, didst thou lions frame,
Since lion vile hath here deflowered my dear?
Which is – no, no, which was – the fairest dame
That lived, that loved, that liked, that looked with cheer.
Come tears, confound;
Out sword and wound

**BOTT/PYRAMUS**   The pap of Pyramus.
Ay, that left pap,
Where heart doth hop.
Thus die I – thus, thus, thus.

*(He stabs himself)*

**BOTT/PYRAMUS**   Now am I dead,
Now am I fled;
My soul is in the sky.
Tongue, lose thy light;
Moon, take thy flight;

*(Exit Starveling)*

**BOTT/PYRAMUS**   Now die, die, die, die, die.

*(He dies. Enter Flute)*

**FLUTE/THISBE**   Asleep, my love?
What, dead, my dove?
O Pyramus, arise.
Speak, speak. Quite dumb?
Dead, dead? A tomb
Must cover thy sweet eyes.
These lily lips,
This cherry nose,
These yellow cowslip cheeks
Are gone, are gone.
Lovers, make moan –
His eyes were green as leeks.
O sisters three,
Come, come to me
With hands as pale as milk;
Lay them in gore,
Since you have shore
With shears his thread of silk.
Tongue, not a word!
Come, trusty sword,
Come blade, my breast imbue.

*(She stabs herself)*

**FLUTE/THISBE**   And farewell friends.
Thus Thisbe ends.
Adieu, adieu, adieu!

*(She dies. The actors face the King and bow before returning to the group)*

| | |
|---|---|
| **KING** | *(Laughing and clapping)* Bravo, more, more! *(Wolf-whistles)* |
| **CHAMBERLAIN** | *(Stunned)* But sire – that was just *awful!* |
| **KING** | It was meant to be, you clot! That was Shakespeare taking the mickey out of actors – jolly funny, if you ask me. |
| **CHAMBERLAIN** | Hilarious, sire. |
| **KING** | Better get a sense of humour, Lord Chamberlain, or I'll have your ribs tickled with a red hot poker. |
| **CHAMBERLAIN** | *(Laughing wildly)* Ha-ha-ha! Good joke, your majesty. |
| **KING** | All right, get on with the show, you lot. I'm still bored. |
| **DIRECTOR** | *(Forward again)* Sire, we go from mirth to madness. In Macbeth, Lady Macbeth persuades her husband to murder the king so that he, Macbeth, will be crowned. But the play goes on to show their terrible guilt. Here, a doctor has been summoned to see the effect of that guilt on Lady Macbeth. |
| | [*Macbeth* V,i] |
| **DOCTOR** | I have two nights watched with you, but can perceive no truth in your report. When was it she last walked? |
| **GENTLEWOMAN** | Since his majesty went into the field, I have seen her rise from her bed, throw her nightgown upon her, unlock her closet, take forth paper, fold it, write upon't, read it, afterwards seal it, and again return to bed yet all this while in a most fast sleep. |
| **DOCTOR** | A great perturbation in nature, to receive at once the benefit of sleep and do the effects of watching. In this slumbery agitation, besides her walking and other actual performances, what at any time have you heard her say? |
| **GENTLEWOMAN** | That, sir, which I will not report after her. |
| **DOCTOR** | You may to me, and 'tis most meet you should. |
| **GENTLEWOMAN** | Neither to you nor anyone, having no witness to confirm my speech. |
| | *(Enter Lady Macbeth with a taper)* |
| **GENTLEWOMAN** | Lo you, here she comes. This is her very guise; and upon my life, fast asleep. Observe her; stand close. |
| **DOCTOR** | How came she by that light? |
| **GENTLEWOMAN** | Why, it stood by her; she has light by her continually, 'tis her command. |

| | |
|---|---|
| **DOCTOR** | You see, her eyes are open. |
| **GENTLEWOMAN** | Ay, but their sense are shut. |
| **DOCTOR** | What is it she does now? Look, how she rubs her hands. |
| **GENTLEWOMAN** | It is an accustomed action with her, to seem thus washing her hands; I have known her continue in this quarter of an hour. |
| **LADY MACBETH** | Yet here's a spot. |
| **DOCTOR** | Hark, she speaks; I will set down what comes from her, to satisfy my remembrance the more strongly. |
| **LADY MACBETH** | Out, damned spot! Out, I say! One, two; why then, 'tis time to do it. Hell is murky! Fie, my lord, fie – a soldier and afeard? What need we fear who knows it, when none can call our power to account? Yet who would have thought the old man to have had so much blood in him. |
| **DOCTOR** | Do you mark that? |
| **LADY MACBETH** | The thane of Fife had a wife; where is she now? What, will these hands ne'er be clean? No more o' that, my lord, no more o' that; you mar all this with starting. |
| **DOCTOR** | Go to, go to; you have known what you should not. |
| **GENTLEWOMAN** | She has spoke what she should not, I am sure of that; heaven knows what she has known. |
| **LADY MACBETH** | Here's the smell of the blood still; all the perfumes of Arabia will not sweeten this little hand. Oh, oh, oh! |
| **DOCTOR** | What a sigh is there! The heart is sorely charged. |
| **GENTLEWOMAN** | I would not have such a heart in my bosom for the dignity of the whole body. |
| **DOCTOR** | Well, well, well. |
| **GENTLEWOMAN** | Pray God it be, sir. |
| **DOCTOR** | This disease is beyond my practice; yet I have known those which have walked in their sleep who have died holily in their beds. |
| **LADY MACBETH** | Wash your hands, put on your nightgown; look not so pale. I tell you yet again, Banquo's buried; he cannot come out on's grave. |
| **DOCTOR** | Even so? |

| | |
|---|---|
| **LADY MACBETH** | To bed, to bed! There's knocking at the gate; come, come, come, come, give me your hand. What's done cannot be undone. To bed, to bed, to bed! |
| | *(Exit Lady Macbeth)* |
| **DOCTOR** | Will she go now to bed? |
| **GENTLEWOMAN** | Directly. |
| **DOCTOR** | Foul whisperings are abroad. Unnatural deeds<br>Do breed unnatural troubles; infected minds<br>To their deaf pillows will discharge their secrets.<br>More needs she the divine than the physician.<br>God, God forgive us all! Look after her;<br>Remove from her the means of all annoyance,<br>And still keep eyes upon her. So, good night;<br>My mind she has mated, and amazed my sight.<br>I think, but dare not speak. |
| **GENTLEWOMAN** | Good night, good doctor. |
| | *(Exit Doctor and Gentlewoman. The actors face the King and bow before returning to the group)* |
| **KING** | Hmmm. Killed a king, did they. |
| **CHAMBERLAIN** | I'm so sorry, your majesty – not the most tactful thing they could have presented. |
| **KING** | On the contrary, Lord Know-it-all. It's a very good lesson – people who kill kings go off their rockers, right? |
| **CHAMBERLAIN** | Right. |
| **KING** | Not that anyone would ever want to kill me.<br>*(Looks behind him)* |
| **DIRECTOR** | *(Who is at the throne now)* Sire. |
| **KING** | *(Starting as he turns back)* Ugh! |
| **DIRECTOR** | Sire, this is our last scene. Appropriately, it is also the last scene of Shakespeare's *Hamlet*. Here's the story so far: |
| | *(Each actor steps forward when he speaks; the other actors form a vignette of what's being described)* |
| **PLAYER 1** | Hamlet's father has died and his mother has, to the disgust of the young Danish Prince, married his uncle – Claudius. |
| | *(Two actors on the point of kissing; the male holds a crown)* |

16

**PLAYER 2**       His father's ghost appears to Hamlet and tells him he was murdered by Claudius.

*(Hamlet kneels before Ghost, who points)*

**PLAYER 3**       Hamlet sets out to discover whether Claudius is really guilty of the murder – or not.

*(Hamlet, still kneeling but now alone, holds his sword aloft)*

**PLAYER 4**       He has a play performed before Claudius; a play in which a king is killed by his brother, who steals his wife and crown as a result.

*(A player takes crown from "poisoned" player)*

**PLAYER 5**       Seeing the play, Claudius can't hide his guilt – but Hamlet kills the Lord Chamberlain, *(reaction from Lord Chamberlain)* Polonius, thinking he is Claudius, and is sent away from Denmark to England.

*(Hamlet stands over Polonius' body with his sword)*

**PLAYER 6**       He returns, but Claudius has stirred up Laertes, Polonius's son, to seek revenge for his father's death.

*(Laertes kneels beside Polonius' body, holding sword aloft as Hamlet did)*

**PLAYER 7**       In our scene, Hamlet and Laertes are about to cross swords in front of Claudius, Hamlet's mother Gertrude and the rest of the court.

*(Hamlet and Laertes face each other, swords drawn)*

**PLAYER 8**       But the audience knows that Laertes' sword has a poisoned tip for killing Hamlet – and that Claudius plans to offer Hamlet a drink he has secretly poisoned.

*(The rest of the actors move into position for the coming scene from Hamlet. Claudius turns away, holding a goblet aloft; Laertes turns away, holding his sword aloft)*

[*Hamlet* V,ii]

**CLAUDIUS**      Come, Hamlet, come, and take this hand from me.

**HAMLET**  Give me your pardon, sir: I have done you wrong;
But pardon't as you are a gentleman.
This presence knows,
And you must needs have heard, how I am punished
With a sore distraction. What I have done,
That might your honour, nature and exception
Roughly awake, I here proclaim was madness.
Let my disclaiming from a purposed evil
Free me so far in your most generous thoughts,
That I have shot my arrow o'er the house,
And hurt my brother.

**LAERTES**  I am satisfied in nature,
Whose motive in this case should stir me most
To my revenge: but in my terms of honour
Stand aloof, and will no reconcilement,
Till by some elder masters of known honour
I have a voice and precedent of peace,
To keep my name ungored. Until that time
I do receive your offered love like love
And will not wrong it.

**HAMLET**  I embrace it freely,
And will this brother's wager frankly play.
Give us the foils: come on.

**LAERTES**  Come, one for me.

**HAMLET**  I'll be your foil, Laertes: in mine ignorance
Your skill shall, like a star i' the darkest night,
Stick fiery off indeed.

**LAERTES**  You mock me, sir.

**HAMLET**  No, by this hand.

**CLAUDIUS**  Give them the foils, young Osric. Cousin Hamlet,
You know the wager?

**HAMLET**  Very well, my lord;
Your grace has laid the odds o' the weaker side.

**CLAUDIUS**  I do not fear it; I have seen you both:
But since he is better, we have therefore odds.

**LAERTES**  This is too heavy; let me see another.

**HAMLET**  This likes me well. These foils have all a length?

**OSRIC**  Ay, my good lord.

*(Hamlet and Laertes prepare to fight)*

| | |
|---|---|
| **CLAUDIUS** | Set me the stoups of wine upon that table. |
| | If Hamlet give the first or second hit, |
| | Or quit in answer of the first exchange, |
| | Let all the battlements their ordnance fire; |
| | The king shall drink to Hamlet's better breath, |
| | And in the cup an union shall he throw, |
| | Richer than that which four successive kings |
| | In Denmark's crown have worn. Give me the cups; |
| | And let the kettle to the trumpet speak, |
| | The trumpet to the cannoneer without, |
| | The cannons to the heavens, the heaven to earth, |
| | "Now the king drinks to Hamlet." Come, begin; |
| | And you, the judges, bear a wary eye. |
| **HAMLET** | Come on, sir. |
| **LAERTES** | Come, my lord. |
| | *(They fight)* |
| **HAMLET** | One. |
| **LAERTES** | No. |
| **HAMLET** | Judgement. |
| **OSRIC** | A hit, a very palpable hit. |
| **LAERTES** | Well, again. |
| **CLAUDIUS** | Stay, give me drink. Hamlet, this pearl is thine; |
| | Here's to thy health; give him the cup. |
| **HAMLET** | I'll play this bout first; set it by a while. |
| | Come. |
| | *(They fight)* |
| **HAMLET** | Another hit, what say you? |
| **LAERTES** | A touch, a touch, I do confess't. |
| **CLAUDIUS** | Our son shall win. |
| **GERTRUDE** | He's fat and scant of breath. |
| | Here, Hamlet, take my napkin, rub thy brows: |
| | The queen carouses to thy fortune, Hamlet. |
| **HAMLET** | Good madam. |
| **CLAUDIUS** | Gertrude do not drink. |
| **GERTRUDE** | I will, my lord; I pray you, pardon me. |

| | |
|---|---|
| **CLAUDIUS** | *(Aside)* It is the poisoned cup; it is too late. |
| **HAMLET** | I dare not drink yet, madam; by and by. |
| **GERTRUDE** | Come, let me wipe they face. |
| **LAERTES** | My lord, I'll hit him now. |
| **CLAUDIUS** | I do not think it. |
| **LAERTES** | *(Aside)* And yet it is almost against my conscience. |
| **HAMLET** | Come for the third, Laertes: you do but dally;<br>I pray you, pass with your best violence;<br>I am sure you make a wanton of me. |
| **LAERTES** | Say you so? Come on.<br><br>*(They fight)* |
| **OSRIC** | Nothing neither way. |
| **LAERTES** | Have at you now!<br><br>*(Laertes wounds Hamlet; in the scuffle they change rapiers and Hamlet wounds Laertes)* |
| **CLAUDIUS** | Part them; they are incensed. |
| **HAMLET** | Nay, come, again.<br><br>*(Gertrude falls. The King pushes the actor playing Claudius out of the way and takes over his role)* |
| **OSRIC** | Look to the Queen there, ho! |
| **HORATIO** | They bleed on both sides. How is it, my lord? |
| **OSRIC** | How is't, Laertes? |
| **LAERTES** | Why, as a woodcock to mine own springe, Osric;<br>I am justly killed with mine own treachery. |
| **HAMLET** | How does the queen? |
| **KING** | She swoons to see them bleed. |
| **GERTRUDE** | No, no, the drink, the drink, O my dear Hamlet,<br>The drink, the drink! I am poisoned.<br><br>*(She dies)* |
| **HAMLET** | O villainy! Ho, let the doors be locked:<br>Treachery, seek it out. |

| | |
|---|---|
| **LAERTES** | It is here, Hamlet. Hamlet, thou art slain;<br>No medicine in the world can do thee good,<br>In thee there is not half an hour's life;<br>The treacherous instrument is in thy hand,<br>Unbated and envenomed: the foul practice<br>Hath turned itself on me; lo, here I lie,<br>Never to rise again: thy mother's poisoned:<br>I can no more: the king, the king's to blame. |
| **HAMLET** | The point envenomed too!<br>Then, venom, to thy work.<br><br>*(Stabs King)* |
| **ALL** | Treason! Treason!<br><br>*(The actors panic, forgetting the play and crowding round the King. The Lord Chamberlain rushes over to the King and checks his pulse)* |
| **CHAMBERLAIN** | *(Horrified)* He's dead.<br><br>*(The actors gape at each other. The King sits bolt upright)* |
| **KING** | Ha! Gotcha! Got the bloomin' lot of you. |
| **CHAMBERLAIN** | Oh your majesty, we thought... |
| **KING** | I know what you thought, you imbecile. Of course I'm not dead – I'm very much alive. |
| **DIRECTOR** | Did you... enjoy it, sire? |
| **KING** | Enjoy it? I haven't had as much fun in years. And that last one, when I was actually in it – well, that was terrific! |
| **DIRECTOR** | Thank you, your majesty. So can we take it you no longer want to... |
| **PLAYER 1** | Torture us... |
| **PLAYER 2** | Hang us... |
| **PLAYER 3** | Draw us... |
| **PLAYER 4** | And quarter us... |
| **PLAYER 5** | And then disembowel us? |

| KING | Of course I don't, idiots! I want to do a play with you – a Shakespearean play. |
|---|---|
| DIRECTOR | Sire – I don't know what to say. |
| KING | Don't say anything then. Yes, we're going to do that Hamlet thing – and I want to be in it. |
| DIRECTOR | Your majesty, we're honoured. Presumably you'd like to be the King again. |

*(They are all trooping off, except the Lord Chamberlain. The King has his arm round the Director's shoulders)*

| KING | Oh no – I want to be Hamlet. |
|---|---|

*(Exit all but Lord Chamberlain. He finds the book of speeches lying on the floor. Picks it up and opens it at the last page. Reads simply)*

[*The Tempest* IV,i]

| CHAMBERLAIN | Our revels now are ended. These our actors, |
|---|---|
| | As I foretold you, were all spirits, and |
| | Are melted into air, into thin air: |
| | And, like the baseless fabric of this vision, |
| | The cloud-capped towers, the gorgeous palaces, |
| | The solemn temples, the great globe itself, |
| | Yea, all which it inherit, shall dissolve |
| | And, like this insubstantial pageant, fade, |
| | Leave not a rack behind. We are such stuff |
| | As dreams are made on, and our little life |
| | Is rounded with a sleep. |

*(Lord Chamberlain closes book and exits)*

# WILL SHAKESPEARE SAVE THE KING!

# WILL SHAKESPEARE SAVE THE KING!

*(Enter Lord Chamberlain)*

**CHAMBERLAIN**    I'm fed up. I'm fed up with being left out. It's not fair.

Where's the King? He's with the Players of course. Can't keep him away from them since he discovered *(With mock reverence)* Shakespeare. No time for the Lord Chamberlain now – spends every minute with them, rehearsing. Ignores me. And it's my birthday tomorrow.

Well I'm fed up with it. I've had enough. I'm going to do something about it. I'm going to KILL HIM! That's right, assassinate the great luvvy. And do you know how I'm going to do it? Funnily enough, I got the idea from Shakespeare – I'm going to poison his drink! He's so wrapped up in his amateur dramatics, he won't suspect a thing – not a thing. And when he's dead, there'll only be one possible successor to the throne – moi! Then we'll see who dares to ignore me. So, make the most of today's rehearsal, your majesty, cos you're heading for your death scene!

*(Lord Chamberlain laughs demonically and then exits. Booing and hissing should be freely encouraged.*

*Enter King, Players and Director. The Players sit round the King and Director, who are centre stage)*

**DIRECTOR**    All right, your maj – it's your big speech. When you're ready.

**KING**    Listen. You may be the Director, but I'm the King. And if you call me "your maj" again, we'll be using your skull for this play instead of that papier-maché one. Clear?

**DIRECTOR**    Crystal. Your majesty.

**KING**    Good.
All the world's a...

**DIRECTOR**    In your own time then. Your majesty.

**KING**    Yes. Thank you.

[*As You Like It* II,vii]

**KING**	All the world's a stage,
And all the men and women merely players:
They have their exits and their entrances
And one man in his time plays many parts,
His acts being seven ages. At first, the infant,
Mewling and puking in the nurse's arms.
And then the whining school-boy, with his satchel
And shining morning face, creeping like snail
Unwillingly to school. And then the lover,
Sighing like furnace, with a woeful ballad
Made to his mistress' eyebrow. Then a soldier,
Full of strange oaths and bearded like the pard,
Jealous in honour, sudden and quick in quarrel,
Seeking the bubble reputation
Even in the cannon's mouth. And then the justice,
In fair round belly with good capon lined,
With eyes severe and beard of formal cut,
Full of wise saws and modern instances;
And so he plays his part. The sixth age shifts
Into the lean and slippered pantaloon,
With spectacles on nose and pouch on side,
His youthful hose, well saved, a world too wide
For his shrunk shank; and his big manly voice
Turning again toward childish treble, pipes
And whistles in his sound. Last scene of all,
That ends this strange eventful history,
Is second childishness and mere oblivion,
Sans teeth, sans eyes, sans taste, sans everything.

*(The Players gape. The King encourages applause. They all applaud frantically)*

**DIRECTOR**	Superb, your majesty.

**KING**	Of course.

**DIRECTOR**	Quite, quite superb.

**KING**	Naturally.

**DIRECTOR**	There is one *tiny* point.

**KING**	What?

**DIRECTOR**	That speech. It isn't actually from *Hamlet*.

**PLAYER 8**	It's from *As You Like It*.

**PLAYER 7**	And we're doing *Hamlet*.

| | |
|---|---|
| **KING** | So. |
| **DIRECTOR** | Well of course it's nothing, your majesty, but as a relative newcomer to the world of the theatre, you may not have realised... |
| **KING** | Realised what? Spit it out, man. In your own time. |
| **DIRECTOR** | When we do a play, we tend to stick to the lines that make up that particular play. |
| **PLAYER 6** | And we're doing *Hamlet*. |
| **PLAYER 7** | Not *As You Like It*. |
| **KING** | So what are you trying to say? You're not telling me I've learnt all that for nothing. |
| **DIRECTOR** | Perhaps we can have a quiet word, your majesty. |
| | *(The King and Director move upstage and the Players gather in the middle.* |
| | *Enter Lord Chamberlain. During the next few lines he creeps up to a goblet and pours poison into it)* |
| **PLAYER 4** | He's such a prima donna, isn't he. |
| **PLAYER 5** | Who, the Director? |
| **PLAYER 4** | No, the King. |
| **PLAYER 1** | Yeah, walks in here as if he owns the place. |
| **PLAYER 3** | Well he does. |
| **PLAYER 1** | Does what? |
| **PLAYER 3** | Own the place. Being the ruler of all he surveys. |
| **PLAYER 1** | Oh. Yeah. |
| **PLAYER 6** | I think it's a great privilege to act with the monarch. I feel very honoured. |
| **THE REST** | Creep! |
| | *(The Lord Chamberlain is creeping off as the King and Director return, parting the crowd of Players)* |
| **DIRECTOR** | That settles it then, your majesty. |
| **KING** | We're doing *As Hamlet Likes It*. |
| **PLAYERS** | What? |

| | |
|---|---|
| **KING** | Oi! Lord Chamberlain. |
| | *(The Lord Chamberlain stops, frozen with guilt. All look round at him)* |
| **KING** | What the hell do you think you're doing? I thought I left you to run the country. |
| **CHAMBERLAIN** | Yes, your majesty, I was just... |
| **KING** | Well, now you're here, you might as well watch. |
| **CHAMBERLAIN** | That's very kind of you, your majesty, but I do have rather a lot of... |
| **KING** | I insist. |
| **CHAMBERLAIN** | *(Sitting)* Fine. |
| **KING** | Good. *(Picking up the goblet)* Director – what's next? |
| **DIRECTOR** | Right, yes, we were going to do the bit where Hamlet meets his old friends, the Players. |
| | *(Response from Players)* |
| **DIRECTOR** | So, places please. |
| | *(The Players group themselves behind the Director)* |
| **DIRECTOR** | Right, from the top! |
| | *(The Director and Players all look expectantly at the King. He stares back. The Lord Chamberlain coughs. The King is about to drink from the goblet)* |
| **PLAYER 6** | *(Sotto voce)* It's you, your majesty. |
| **KING** | What? |
| **PLAYER 7** | It's you – your line. |
| **KING** | Oh, right! Me, my line, yes – sorry, sorry. Right, here we go. |
| | *(He thinks, visibly)* |
| **PLAYER 4** | He's forgotten it. |
| **PLAYER 5** | He never learnt it. |
| **PLAYER 6** | He's doing his best. |
| **THE REST** | Creep! |
| **KING** | Look, sorry, everyone – I don't know it. |
| | *(He is about to drink)* |

| | |
|---|---|
| **DIRECTOR** | Your majesty: |
| | [*Hamlet* III,ii] |
| | Speak the speech, I pray you, as I pronounced it to you, trippingly on the tongue: but if you mouth it, as many of our players do, I had as lief the town crier spoke my lines. Nor do not saw the air too much with your hand, thus, but use all gently; for in the very torrent, tempest and, as I may say, whirlwind of your passion, you must acquire and beget a temperance that may give it smoothness. |
| | Be not too tame, neither, but let your own discretion be your tutor; suit the action to the word, the word to the action, with this special observance – that you o'erstep not the modesty of nature. For anything so o'erdone is from the purpose of playing, whose end, both at the first and now, was and is, to hold, as 'twere, a mirror up to nature: to show virtue her own feature, scorn her own image, and the very age and body of the time his form and pressure. |
| **KING** | OK, thanks for the advice – now, could you tell me what my speech is. |
| **DIRECTOR** | Your majesty – that *was* your speech. |
| **KING** | Was it? Of course it was. I knew that. *You* could never come out with anything as good as that. Right, so, how did it start? Say the lines... ? |
| **DIRECTOR** | Speak the speech... |
| **PLAYER 1** | He doesn't know it. |
| **PLAYER 2** | He'll never learn it. |
| **PLAYER 4** | He's holding us up. |
| **PLAYER 5** | He's letting us down. |
| **PLAYER 6** | I must admit, he isn't doing very well. |
| | *(All the Players look hard at Player 6.* |
| | *Meanwhile the King has been struggling to remember his lines. At last, he gives up and throws his arms wide in a gesture of resignation. The poisoned drink flies out of the goblet and all over the Lord Chamberlain. The Director and Players burst out laughing)* |

| | |
|---|---|
| **CHAMBERLAIN** | Oh ha-ha-ha! |
| | *(The Lord Chamberlain suddenly realises that poison may have entered his mouth)* |
| **CHAMBERLAIN** | *(Running off and spitting)* No! NO! Not ME! |
| | *(Exit Lord Chamberlain)* |
| **KING** | What on earth's got into him? |
| **DIRECTOR** | I know not, your majesty – but I suggest we all take five. Take five, everyone. |
| | *(Exit the Players)* |
| **KING** | Take five what? |
| **DIRECTOR** | Minutes, sire. Have a break, a rest, a royal recuperation. |
| **KING** | Yes all right, I'm not completely stupid. |
| | *(Exit Director)* |
| **KING** | *(Calling after him)* I can still have your head cut off, you know! |
| | *(The King sits, picks up the book of Shakespeare and begins flipping through it)* |
| **KING** | Now, where's this speech? (Yawns) Ah, here we are. |
| | *(He lies down, holding the book up and reading)* |
| **KING** | Speak the speech, I pray you, as I pronounced it to you, trippingly on the tongue. |
| | *(He puts the book on his chest and yawns again)* |
| **KING** | Right. Speak the speech... I pray you... as I... *(Checks book)* pronounced, that's it, as I pronounced it to you... *(He is falling asleep)* trippingly on the... trippingly on the... |
| | *(He is asleep and starts to snore. He turns over on his side, facing the audience; the book slides to the floor. Enter the Lord Chamberlain)* |
| **CHAMBERLAIN** | Your maj... |
| | *(Lord Chamberlain stops and stares. The King snorts in his sleep. The Lord Chamberlain slowly, stealthily approaches the King and walks round behind him. Suddenly he produces a small bottle of poison, holds it up and then kisses it. He takes off the lid and is bending to pour it in the royal ear when the King jerks upright, knocking the Lord Chamberlain flying)* |

| | |
|---|---|
| **KING** | *(Still half-asleep)* Worrappen? *(After shaking his head)* I must have fallen asleep. |
| | *(He sees Lord Chamberlain and stands over him)* |
| **KING** | Lord Chamberlain – what on earth are you doing? |
| **CHAMBERLAIN** | *(Sitting up and stammering)* Well, your majesty, I was just... |
| **KING** | Well stop it. |
| | *(He starts to go, but turns suddenly)* |
| **KING** | Hey, I've just remembered something. |
| **CHAMBERLAIN** | Sire? |
| **KING** | None of your business. |
| | *(Exit King. Lord Chamberlain limps downstage and faces the audience)* |
| | [*Richard III* I,i] |
| **CHAMBERLAIN** | Now is the winter of our discontent<br>Made glorious summer by this sun of York;<br>And all the clouds that loured upon our house<br>In the deep bosom of the ocean buriéd.<br>Now are our brows bound with victorious wreaths;<br>Our bruiséd arms hung up for monuments;<br>Our stern alarums changed to merry meetings,<br>Our dreadful marches to delightful measures.<br>Grim-visaged war hath smoothed his wrinkled front;<br>And now, instead of mounting barbéd steeds<br>To fright the souls of fearful adversaries,<br>He capers nimbly in a lady's chamber<br>To the lascivious pleasing of a lute.<br>But I, that am not shaped for sportive tricks,<br>Nor made to court an amorous looking-glass;<br>I, that am rudely stamped, and want love's majesty<br>To strut before a wanton ambling nymph;<br>I, that am curtailed of this fair proportion,<br>Cheated of feature by dissembling nature,<br>Deformed, unfinished, sent before my time<br>Into this breathing world scarce half made up,<br>And that so lamely and unfashionable<br>That dogs bark at me as I halt by them; |

| | |
|---|---|
| **CHAMBERLAIN** | Why I, in this weak piping time of peace, |
| | Have no delight to pass away the time, |
| | Unless to spy my shadow in the sun |
| | And descant on mine own deformity: |
| | And therefore, since I cannot prove a lover, |
| | To entertain these fair well-spoken days, |
| | I am determined to prove a villain |
| | And hate the idle pleasures of these days. |

You see. It's not just them that can strut and fret with old Shakespeare. But are they interested in what I have to offer? Oh no, not me, not the Lord Chamberlain – he's nobody. And no-one remembers a nobody's birthday.

*(Exit Lord Chamberlain, sniffling.*

*Enter, from the opposite side, the King followed by the Director and Players)*

**KING**      And then I suddenly remembered – *(He looks around, checking for the Lord Chamberlain)* it's all right, he's gone now – I suddenly remembered, it's his birthday *tomorrow*.

**THE REST**      Party!

**KING**      Yes, yes, all right, we'll have a party. But the thing is, I've been neglecting the old clot recently – and I'd like to do something really *special* for him.

**DIRECTOR**      Have his head cut off, majesty?

**KING**      Yes! No! Don't be facetious.

**DIRECTOR**      So what did you have in mind, sire?

**KING**      Um... dunno.

**PLAYER 3**      Tell you what – we could do what we did for you.

**PLAYER 6**      When you were bored.

**PLAYER 7**      *Really* bored.

**PLAYER 8**      And you threatened to have us hung.

**PLAYER 1**      Drawn.

**PLAYER 2**      And quartered.

**DIRECTOR**      That's it, sire – scenes from Shakespeare.

| | |
|---|---|
| **KING** | A special birthday presentation – what a brilliant idea. Of mine. |
| **PLAYER 8** | There is one slight problem. |
| **KING**<br>**DIRECTOR** | What? |
| **PLAYER 8** | Well, we've been rehearsing *As Hamlet Likes It* all the time. We haven't got any scenes ready. |
| **PLAYER 1** | What about the ones we did before? |
| **PLAYER 4** | No, he's *seen* them. |
| **DIRECTOR** | But my dears, the answer is obvious – we do scenes from *Ham* – I mean, *As You* – from the play we've been working on. |
| **KING** | No, can't do that. |
| **DIRECTOR** | Why not? |
| **KING** | Because it's all too miserable. We want to cheer him up, not drive him to drink. |
| **PLAYER 3** | We've got a scene. |
| **PLAYER 7** | It's from *Twelfth Night*. |
| **DIRECTOR** | And *who* directed it? |
| **PLAYER 3** | Um, we did. |
| **PLAYER 7** | Just for practice. |
| **PLAYER 3** | You see, we've only got small parts in... |
| **DIRECTOR** | Silence! We are not presenting anything that *I* haven't directed. |
| **KING** | Oh rubbish! Come on, let's see it. |
| **PLAYER 3** | Thank you, your majesty. |
| **PLAYER 7** | The situation is this. Viola, the heroine, is disguised as a eunuch called Cesario. In this disguise, she serves the duke, Orsino. |
| **PLAYER 3** | Orsino sends Viola to see the woman he loves, Olivia. But Olivia isn't interested in Orsino – as you'll see. |

[*Twelfth Night* III,i]

**VIOLA**

My duty, madam, and most humble service.

**OLIVIA**

What is your name?

**VIOLA**

Cesario is your servant's name, fair princess.

**OLIVIA**

You're servant to the Count Orsino, youth.

**VIOLA**

And he is yours and his must needs be yours:
Your servant's servant is your servant, madam.

**OLIVIA**

For him, I think not on him: for his thoughts,
Would they were blanks, rather than filled with me.

**VIOLA**

Madam, I come to whet your gentle thoughts
On his behalf.

**OLIVIA**

O, by your leave, I pray you,
I bade you never speak again of him:
But, would you undertake another suit,
I had rather hear you to solicit that
Than music from the spheres.

**VIOLA**

Dear lady –

**OLIVIA**

Give me leave, I beseech you. I did send,
After the last enchantment you did here,
A ring in chase of you: so did I abuse
Myself, my servant and, I fear me, you.
Under your hard construction must I sit,
To force that on you, in a shameful cunning,
Which you knew none of yours: what might you think?
Have you not set mine honour at the stake
And baited it with all the unmuzzled thoughts
That tyrannous heart can think? To one of your receiving
Enough is shown. So, let me hear you speak.

**VIOLA**

I pity you.

**OLIVIA**

That's a degree to love.

**VIOLA**

No, not a grize; for 'tis a vulgar proof,
That very oft we pity enemies.

**OLIVIA**

Why then, methinks 'tis time to smile again.
O world, how apt the poor are to be proud.
Be not afraid, good youth, I will not have you:
And yet, when wit and youth is come to harvest,
Your wife is like to reap a proper man:
There lies your way, due west.

| | |
|---|---|
| **VIOLA** | Then westward-ho! Grace and good disposition<br>Attend your ladyship.<br>You'll nothing, madam, to my lord by me? |
| **OLIVIA** | Stay.<br>I prithee, tell me what thou thinkst of me. |
| **VIOLA** | That you do think you are not what you are. |
| **OLIVIA** | If I think so, I think the same of you. |
| **VIOLA** | Then think you right; I am not what I am. |
| **OLIVIA** | I would you were as I would have you be. |
| **VIOLA** | Would it be better, madam, than I am?<br>I wish it might, for now I am your fool. |
| **OLIVIA** | O, what a deal of scorn looks beautiful<br>In the contempt and anger of his lip.<br>A murderous guilt shows not itself more soon<br>Than love that would seem hid: love's night is noon.<br>Cesario, by the roses of the spring,<br>By maidhood, honour, truth and every thing,<br>I love thee, so that, maugre all thy pride,<br>Nor wit nor reason can my passion hide.<br>Do not extort thy reasons from this clause,<br>For that I woo; thou therefore hast no cause;<br>But rather reason thus with reason fetter –<br>Love sought is good, but given unsought, better. |
| **VIOLA** | By innocence, I swear, and by my youth,<br>I have one heart, one bosom and one truth,<br>And that no woman has; nor never none<br>Shall mistress be of it, save I alone.<br>And so adieu, good madam: never more<br>Will I my master's tears to you deplore. |
| **OLIVIA** | Yet come again; for thou perhaps mayst move<br>That heart, which now abhors to like his love. |
| | *(The two Players bow. All applaud)* |
| **KING** | Hmm, well, it's still too miserable. We want something funny. |
| **DIRECTOR** | Then we'd better look in the book. |
| **KING** | Book? What book? |
| **THE REST** | *(Holding it in front of him)* Shakespeare! |
| **KING** | Oh. Yes. That book. |

| | |
|---|---|
| **DIRECTOR** | It's the Lord Chamberlain's birthday tomorrow. That means we've only got twelve hours. So we've got to work hard, and we've got to work fast. Right? |
| **THE REST** | Right! |
| **DIRECTOR** | Good! Now, first we pick our scenes. |
| | *(They all huddle round the book; there is a brief burst of indistinct discussion, then quiet)* |
| **KING** | Right, that's settled then. |
| **PLAYER 1** | But *you* chose them all. |
| **KING** | Exactly. I'm King. |
| **DIRECTOR** | Now, we choose a cast. |
| | *(As before: huddle, hubbub, quiet)* |
| **KING** | Right. Sorted. |
| **PLAYER 2** | But *you've* got all the best parts. |
| **KING** | Exactly. I'm King. |
| **DIRECTOR** | Now, we learn our lines. |
| | *(Time passes. All can be seen to be learning their lines)* |
| **KING** | Right. Done that. |
| **PLAYER 4** | *(Quietly)* Bet he doesn't know his lines. |
| **KING** | *(Overhearing)* You know, you're absolutely right. But I can get away with it – know why? |
| **THE REST** | You're King! |
| **KING** | Exactly. |
| **DIRECTOR** | Now, we rehearse. |

*(Mimed rehearsal sequence giving hints of the scenes to be presented and including the usual arguments. The actors slow down gradually until eventually they drop in slow motion to the floor and into sleep. The King thrusts the book of Shakespeare inside his cloak as if he can learn his lines by osmosis.*

*Enter Lord Chamberlain with a foil and a bottle of poison. He removes the lid and dips the foil's point into the poison. He creeps up to the sleeping King and, after looking round, tries to stab him – but his foil just bends)*

| KING | (*Jerking awake*) Lord Chamberlain, what on earth are you doing? You stabbed me right in the Shakespeare. |
|---|---|
| | (*The King pulls the book from his cloak. The Lord Chamberlain is stunned*) |
| THE REST | (*Jumping up*) Surprise! |
| KING | (*To Lord Chamberlain*) That's right, you old fool – surprise! Surprised? |
| CHAMBERLAIN | Well, your majesty, I... |
| KING | Hang on, though, before we forget – happy birthday! |
| THE REST | Happy birthday! |
| | (*The Director assumes a conductor's pose*) |
| DIRECTOR | Right, after three – three! |
| ALL | **(Singing)** Happy birthday to you, Happy birthday to you, Happy birthday, Lord Chamberlain, Happy birthday to you. |
| | (*A cake is brought in; the Lord Chamberlain is overwhelmed*) |
| KING | And that's not all, my dear idiot-chum! Mr. Director, over to you. |
| DIRECTOR | Thank you, your majesty. Lord Chamberlain, we'd like to present, in honour of your birthday, two scenes from Shakespeare. |
| PLAYER 1 | The first is from *Much Ado About Nothing*. |
| PLAYER 2 | In this scene, we see how Benedick is trapped into loving Beatrice. |
| | [*Much Ado About Nothing* II,iii] |
| BENEDICK | Boy! |
| BOY | Signior? |
| BENEDICK | In my chamber window lies a book: bring it hither to me in the orchard. |
| BOY | I am here already, sir. |
| BENEDICK | I know that; but I would have thee hence and here again. |
| | (*Exit Boy*) |

| **BENEDICK** | I do much wonder that one man, seeing how much another man is a fool when he dedicates his behaviours to love, will, after he hath laughed at such shallow follies in others, become the argument of his own scorn by falling in love: and such a man is Claudio. I have known when there was no music with him but the drum and the fife: and now he had rather hear the tabor and the pipe. I have known when he would have walked ten mile afoot to see a good armour: and now will he lie ten nights awake, carving the fashion of a new doublet. He was wont to speak plain and to the purpose, like an honest man and a soldier; and now is he turned orthography, his words are a very fantastical banquet. May I be so converted and see with these eyes? I cannot tell. I think not. I will not be sworn but love may transform me to an oyster; but I'll take my oath on it, till he have made an oyster of me, he shall never make me such a fool. One woman is fair, yet I am well; another is wise, yet I am well; another virtuous, yet I am well; but till all graces be in one woman, one woman shall not come in my grace. Rich she shall be, that's certain; wise, or I'll none; virtuous, or I'll never cheapen her; fair, or I'll never look on her; mild, or come not near me; of good discourse, an excellent musician and her hair shall be... of what colour it please God. Ha! The Prince and Monsieur Love. I will hide me in the arbour. |
|---|---|
| | *(He hides. Enter Don Pedro, Claudio and Leonato)* |
| **DON PEDRO** | See you where Benedick hath hid himself? |
| **CLAUDIO** | O very well, my lord. |
| **DON PEDRO** | Come hither, Leonato. What was it you told me of today? That your niece Beatrice was in love with Signior Benedick? |
| **CLAUDIO** | I did never think that lady would have loved any man. |
| **LEONATO** | No, nor I neither; but most wonderful that she should so dote on Signior Benedick, whom she hath in all outward behaviours seemed ever to abhor. |
| **BENEDICK** | Is't possible? |
| **LEONATO** | By my troth, my lord, I cannot tell what to think of it but that she loves him with an enraged affection. |
| **DON PEDRO** | Maybe she doth but counterfeit. |
| **CLAUDIO** | Faith, like enough. |
| **LEONATO** | O God, counterfeit! There was never counterfeit of passion came so near the life of passion as she discovers it. |

| | |
|---|---|
| **DON PEDRO** | Why, what effects of passion shows she? |
| **LEONATO** | What effects, my lord? You heard my daughter tell you. |
| **CLAUDIO** | She did indeed. |
| **DON PEDRO** | You amaze me. I would have thought her spirit had been invincible against all assaults of affection. |
| **LEONATO** | I would have sworn it had, my lord. Especially against Benedick. |
| **DON PEDRO** | Hath she made her affection known to Benedick? |
| **LEONATO** | No, and swears she never will. That's her torment. |
| **CLAUDIO** | 'Tis true indeed; so your daughter says. "Shall I," says she "that have so oft encountered him with scorn, write to him that I love him?" |
| **LEONATO** | This says she now when she is beginning to write to him; for she'll be up twenty times a night, and there will sit in her smock till she have writ a sheet of paper – my daughter tells us all. |
| **CLAUDIO** | Now you talk of a sheet of paper, I remember a pretty jest your daughter told us of. |
| **LEONATO** | Oh. When she had writ it and was reading it over, she found Benedick and Beatrice between the sheets. Oh, she tore the letter, railed at herself that she should be so immodest to write to one that she knew would flout her. |
| **CLAUDIO** | Then down upon her knees she falls, weeps, sobs, beats her heart, tears her hair, prays, curses: "O sweet Benedick! God give me patience!" |
| **LEONATO** | She doth indeed – my daughter says so – and the ecstasy hath so much overborne her that my daughter is sometime afeard that she will do a desperate outrage to herself: it is very true. |
| **DON PEDRO** | It were good that Benedick knew of it by some other, if she will not discover it. |
| **CLAUDIO** | To what end? He would make but a sport of it and torment the poor lady worse. |
| **DON PEDRO** | If he should, it were an alms to hang him. She's an excellent sweet lady and, out of all suspicion, she is virtuous. |
| **CLAUDIO** | And she is exceeding wise. |

**DON PEDRO**    In every thing but in loving Benedick. I love him well, and I could wish he would modestly examine himself, to see how much he is unworthy so good a lady.

**LEONATO**    My lord, will you walk? Dinner is ready.

*(Exit Don Pedro, Claudio and Leonato)*

**BENEDICK**    This can be no trick; the conference was sadly borne. They have the truth of this from Hero. They seem to pity the lady; it seems her affections have their full bent. Love me! Why, it must be requited! I hear how I am censured. They say I will bear myself proudly, if I perceive the love come from her. They say too that she will rather die than give any sign of affection. I did never think to marry. I must not seem proud; happy are they that hear their detractions and can put them to mending. They say the lady is fair; 'tis a truth, I can bear them witness. And virtuous: 'tis so, I cannot reprove it. And wise, but for loving me: by my troth, it is no addition to her wit, nor no great argument of her folly, for I will be horribly in love with her. I may chance have some odd quirks and remnants of wit broken on me, because I have railed so long against marriage; but doth not the appetite alter? The world must be peopled. When I said I would die a bachelor, I did not think I would live till I were married. Here comes Beatrice. By this day, she's a fair lady! I do spy some marks of love in her.

*(Enter Beatrice)*

**BEATRICE**    Against my will I am sent to bid you come in to dinner.

**BENEDICK**    Fair Beatrice, I thank you for your pains.

**BEATRICE**    I took no more pains for those thanks than you took pains to thank me; if it had been painful I would not have come.

**BENEDICK**    You take pleasure then in the message?

**BEATRICE**    Yea, just so much as you may take upon a knife's point. Fare you well.

*(Exit Beatrice)*

**BENEDICK**    Ha! "Against my will I am sent to bid you come in to dinner". There's a double meaning in that. "I took no more pains for those thanks than you took pains to thank me." That's as much as to say, any pains that I take for you is as easy as thanks. If I do not take pity of her, I am a villain. If I do not love her, I am a Jew. I will go get her picture.

(The Players bow and the Lord Chamberlain applauds)

**CHAMBERLAIN**  (Moved) Thank you, thank you, thank you all so much.

**KING**  Well don't go over the top yet – there's another one to go. Director.

**DIRECTOR**  Thank you, sire. Our final scene is from *Henry IV, Part One,* and...

**CHAMBERLAIN**  Oh!

(All turn and stare at him)

**KING**  What on earth's the matter, Lord Chamberlain?

**CHAMBERLAIN**  Nothing, your majesty.

**DIRECTOR**  It's taken from Act II, scene iv...

**CHAMBERLAIN**  Oh!

(All stare again)

**KING**  Are you all right, Lord Chamberlain?

**CHAMBERLAIN**  Yes, your majesty – it's nothing, really.

**DIRECTOR**  The story so far.

**PLAYER 5**  Fat Jack Falstaff and his friends have robbed some travellers.

**PLAYER 6**  But Prince Hal and Poins have, in turn, robbed Falstaff and his men.

**PLAYER 7**  They all meet up in the pub.

**PLAYER 8**  And Falstaff begins to tell the Prince and Poins what happened.

(The King has put on some padding to play Falstaff. The Director plays Hal. The Lord Chamberlain comes forward)

**CHAMBERLAIN**  Your majesty, may I speak?

**KING**  Not *now*, Lord Chamberlain, we're about to do the scene.

**CHAMBERLAIN**  The thing is, your majesty, I've been feeling rather left out of all this Shakespeare hoo-hah...

**KING**  Yes, yes, we know – that's why we're doing this.

**CHAMBERLAIN**  And I've actually learnt a few speeches and scenes myself.

**KING**  Splendid. Now sit down, there's a good...

**CHAMBERLAIN**  And one of the parts I know is Falstaff. In this scene.

| | |
|---|---|
| **KING** | But *I'm* playing Falstaff. |
| **CHAMBERLAIN** | *(Sitting)* Yes of course, your majesty. Sorry for mentioning it. |
| **THE REST** | But it's his birthday. |
| | *(The King deliberates)* |
| **KING** | *(Removing padding)* Oh, all right then – you can play Falstaff. |
| **CHAMBERLAIN** | Oh your majesty! |
| **KING** | Transfer the padding. |
| | *(The padding is transferred)* |
| **KING** | Right – go! |
| | [*Henry IV, Part One* II,iv] |
| | *(Enter Falstaff, Gadshill, Bardolph, Peto and Francis)* |
| **POINS** | Welcome, Jack. Where hast thou been? |
| **FALSTAFF** | A plague of all cowards, I say, and a vengeance too! Give me a cup of sack, boy. *(Drinks)* You rogue, here's lime in this sack. There's nothing but roguery to be found in villainous man – yet a coward is worse than a cup of sack with lime in it. A villainous coward! Go thy ways, old Jack, die when thou wilt; if manhood, good manhood, be not forgot upon the face of the earth, then I am a shotten herring. There live not three good men unhanged in England, and one of them is fat and grows old. God help the while – a bad world, I say. A plague of all cowards, I still say. |
| **PRINCE** | How now, wool-sack. What mutter you? |
| **FALSTAFF** | A king's son! If I do not beat thee out of thy kingdom with a dagger, and drive all thy subjects afore thee like a flock of wild geese, I'll never wear hair on my face more. You, Prince of Wales! |
| **PRINCE** | Why you whoreson round man. What's the matter? |
| **FALSTAFF** | Are not you a coward? Answer me that. And Poins there. |
| **POINS** | Zounds, you fat paunch, if you call me coward, by the Lord, I'll stab thee. |
| **FALSTAFF** | I call thee coward! I'll see thee damned ere I call thee coward. But I would give a thousand pounds if I could run as fast as thou canst. A plague of all cowards, still say I. |
| **PRINCE** | What's the matter? |

| | |
|---|---|
| **FALSTAFF** | What's the matter! There be four of us have taken a thousand pounds this day morning. |
| **PRINCE** | Where is it, Jack? Where is it? |
| **FALSTAFF** | Where is it! Taken from us, it is: a hundred upon four of us. |
| **PRINCE** | What, a hundred, man? |
| **FALSTAFF** | I am a rogue if I were not at half-sword with a dozen of them two hours together. I have 'scaped by a miracle. I am eight times thrust through the doublet, four through the hose; my buckler cut through and through; my sword hacked like a hand-saw. I never dealt better since I was a man. A plague of all cowards! Let them speak; if they speak more or less than truth, they are villains and the sons of darkness. |
| **PRINCE** | Speak, sirs. How was it? |
| **GADSHILL** | We four set upon some dozen... |
| **FALSTAFF** | Sixteen at least, my lord. |
| **GADSHILL** | And bound them. |
| **PETO** | No, no, they were not bound. |
| **FALSTAFF** | You rogue, they were bound, every man of them. |
| **GADSHILL** | Some six or seven fresh men set upon us... |
| **FALSTAFF** | And unbound the rest, and then come in the other. |
| **PRINCE** | What, fought you with them all? |
| **FALSTAFF** | All! I know not what you call all – but if I fought not with fifty of them, I am a bunch of radish. If there were not two or three and fifty upon poor old Jack, then I am no two-legged creature. |
| **PRINCE** | Pray God you have not murdered some of them. |
| **FALSTAFF** | Nay, that's past praying for. I have peppered two of them; two I am sure I have paid, two rogues in buckram suits. I tell thee what, Hal, if I tell thee a lie, spit in my face, call me horse. Four rogues in buckram let drive at me... |
| **PRINCE** | What, four? Thou saidst but two even now. |

| | |
|---|---|
| **FALSTAFF** | Four, Hal. I told thee four. |
| **POINS** | Ay, ay, he said four. |
| **FALSTAFF** | These four came all a-front, and mainly thrust at me. I made me no more ado but took all their seven points in my target, thus. |
| **PRINCE** | Seven? Why there were but four even now. |
| **FALSTAFF** | In buckram? |
| **POINS** | Ay, four in buckram suits. |
| **FALSTAFF** | Seven, by these hilts, or I am a villain else. |
| **PRINCE** | Prithee, let him alone. We shall have more anon. |
| **FALSTAFF** | Dost thou hear me, Hal? |
| **PRINCE** | Ay, and mark thee too, Jack. |
| **FALSTAFF** | Do so, for it is worth the listening to. These nine in buckram that I told thee of... |
| **PRINCE** | So, two more already. |
| **FALSTAFF** | Their points being broken... |
| **POINS** | Down fell their hose. |
| **FALSTAFF** | Began to give me ground. But I followed me close, came in foot and hand; and with a thought, seven of the eleven I paid. |
| **PRINCE** | O monstrous! Eleven buckram men grown out of two! |
| **FALSTAFF** | But as the devil would have it, three misbegotten knaves in Kendal green came at my back and let drive at me; for it was so dark, Hal, that thou couldst not see thy hand. |
| **PRINCE** | These lies are like their father that begets them: gross as a mountain, open, palpable. Why, thou clay-brained guts, thou knotty-pated fool, thou whoreson, obscene, greasy tallow-catch... |
| **FALSTAFF** | What, art thou mad? Art thou mad? Is not the truth the truth? |
| **PRINCE** | Why, how couldst thou know these men in Kendal green, when it was so dark thou couldst not see thy hand? Come, tell us your reason. What sayest thou to this? |

| | |
|---|---|
| **POINS** | Come, your reason, Jack, your reason. |
| **FALSTAFF** | What, upon compulsion! If reasons were as plentiful as blackberries, I would give no man a reason upon compulsion, I. |
| **PRINCE** | I'll be no longer guilty of this sin. This sanguine coward, this bed-presser, this horseback-breaker, this huge hill of flesh... |
| **FALSTAFF** | 'Sblood, you starveling, you elf-skin, you dried neat's tongue, you bull's pizzle, you stockfish! O for breath to utter what is like thee! You tailor's-yard, you sheath, you bow-case, you vile standing-tuck... |
| **PRINCE** | Well, breathe awhile and then to it again, and when thou hast tired thyself in base comparisons, hear me speak but this. |
| **POINS** | Mark, Jack. |
| **PRINCE** | We two saw you four set on four and bound them, and were masters of their wealth. Mark now, how a plain tale shall put you down. Then did we two set on you four, and with a word out-faced you from your prize, and have it, yea, and can show it you here in the house. And Falstaff, you carried your guts away as nimbly, with as quick dexterity, and roared for mercy and still run and roared, as ever I heard bull-calf. What a slave art thou, to hack thy sword as thou hast done, and then say it was in fight! What trick, what device, what starting-hole, canst thou now find out to hide thee from this open and apparent shame? |
| **POINS** | Come, let's hear, Jack. What trick hast thou now? |
| **FALSTAFF** | By the Lord, I knew ye as well as He that made ye. Why, hear you, my masters – was it for me to kill the heir-apparent? Should I turn upon the true prince? Why, thou knowest I am as valiant as Hercules – but beware instinct. The lion will not touch the true prince. Instinct is a great matter; I was a coward on instinct. I shall think the better of myself and thee during my life; I for a valiant lion, and thou for a true prince. But, by the Lord, lads, I am glad you have the money. |
| | *(All bow to the King)* |
| **KING** | *(Grudgingly)* Well done, everyone. Especially you, Lord Chamberlain – very good. In fact, I suppose I couldn't have done better myself. |

| | |
|---|---|
| **ALL** | Hurrah! |
| **CHAMBERLAIN** | Thank you, your majesty. |
| **KING** | *(To the Director and Players)* All right, you lot – go and get the party going. |
| | *(Exit the Players, whooping and yelling. The Director is stalking off in a huff)* |
| **KING** | Oh and you were excellent too, Director. |
| | *(The Director turns and checks round him, as if he can't believe the praise could possibly be for him)* |
| **DIRECTOR** | Moi? |
| **CHAMBERLAIN** | Yes, you really were. *(Shaking his hand)* A pleasure working with you. |
| **DIRECTOR** | Likewise, darling, likewise. |
| | *(Exit Director, whooping and yelling)* |
| **KING** | Happy now? |
| **CHAMBERLAIN** | Oh yes, sire. This is the best birthday I've... |
| **KING** | Oh pur-lease! Lord Chamberlain, I'd like to apologise for having ignored you all this time... |
| **CHAMBERLAIN** | Oh, sire. |
| **KING** | I'd like to, but seeing as I'm King, I can't start grovelling to the likes of you, so I won't. Still, it's the thought that counts. |
| **CHAMBERLAIN** | Yes, your majesty. |
| **KING** | *(Putting an arm round the Lord Chamberlain's shoulders)* Now, let's hit the party. |
| | *(They start to go. The King stops)* |
| **KING** | Oh and one other thing, Lord Chamberlain. |
| **CHAMBERLAIN** | Sire? |
| **KING** | You know I don't like violence, but if you ever try to assassinate me again, I'll have your entire body scooped out and stuffed so we can use you in stunt routines. OK? |
| | *(Lord Chamberlain nods weakly)* |

| KING | Splendid! Shall we go? |
|---|---|

*(Exit the King and Lord Chamberlain. Enter a female Player, who looks for the book, finds it and reads:)*

[*As You Like It* – Epilogue]

| PLAYER | It is not the fashion to see the lady the epilogue; but it is no more unhandsome than to see the lord the prologue. What a case am I in then, that am neither a good epilogue nor cannot insinuate with you in the behalf of a good play. I am not furnished like a beggar, therefore to beg will not become me. My way is to conjure you; and I'll begin with the women. I charge you, O women, for the love you bear to men, to like as much of this play as please you. And I charge you, O men, for the love you bear to women – as I perceive by your simpering that none of you hates them – that between you and the women the play may please. If I were a woman I would kiss as many of you as had beards that pleased me, complexions that liked me and breaths that I defied not. And, I am sure, as many as have good beards or good faces or sweet breaths will, for my kind offer, when I make curtsy, bid me farewell. |
|---|---|

## ADDITIONAL TITLES AVAILABLE

All books may be ordered direct from:

DRAMATIC LINES   PO BOX 201   TWICKENHAM   TW2 5RQ   ENGLAND

freefone:  0800 5429570
fax: 020 8296 9503
www.dramaticlines.co.uk

## THE SIEVE
### AND OTHER SCENES
**Heather Stephens**
ISBN 0 9522224 0 X

The Sieve contains unusual short original monologues valid for junior acting examinations. The material in The Sieve has proved popular with winning entries worldwide in drama festival competitions. Although these monologues were originally written for the 8-14 year age range they have been used by adult actors for audition and performance pieces. Each monologue is seen through the eyes of a young person with varied subject matter including tough social issues such as fear, 'Television Spinechiller', senile dementia , 'Seen Through a Glass Darkly' and withdrawal from the world in 'The Sieve'. Other pieces include: 'A Game of Chicken', 'The Present', 'Balloon Race' and a widely used new adaptation of Hans Christian Andersen's 'The Little Match Girl' in monologue form.

## CABBAGE
### AND OTHER SCENES
**Heather Stephens**
ISBN 0 9522224 5 0

Following the success of The Sieve, Heather Stephens has written an additional book of monologues with thought provoking and layered subject matter valid for junior acting examinations. The Cabbage monologues were originally written for the 8-14 year age range but have been used by adult actors for audition and performance pieces. The Aberfan slag heap disaster issues are graphically confronted in 'Aberfan Prophecy' and 'The Surviving Twin' whilst humorous perceptions of life are observed by young people in 'The Tap Dancer' and 'Cabbage'. Other pieces include: 'The Dinner Party Guest', 'Nine Lives' and a new adaptation of Robert Browning's 'The Pied Piper' seen through the eyes of the crippled child.

## ALONE IN MY ROOM
### ORIGINAL MONOLOGUES
**Ken Pickering**
ISBN 0 9537770 0 6

This collection of short original monologues includes extracts from the author's longer works in addition to the classics. Provocative issues such as poverty and land abuse are explored in 'One Child at a Time', 'The Young Person Talks' and 'Turtle Island' with adaptations from 'Jane Eyre', Gulliver's Travels' and 'Oliver Twist' and well loved authors include Dostoyevsky. These monologues have a wide variety of applications including syllabus recommendation for various acting examinations. Each monologue has a brief background description and acting notes.

# DUOLOGUES

## PEARS

Heather Stephens
ISBN 0 9522224 6 9

These thought provoking and unusual short original duologues provide new material for speech and drama festival candidates in the 8-14 year age range. The scenes have also been widely used for junior acting examinations and in a variety of school situations and theatrical applications. Challenging topics in Pears include the emotive issues of child migration, 'Blondie', 'The Outback Institution' and bullying 'Bullies', other scenes examine friendship, 'The Best of Friends', 'The Row' and envy, 'Never the Bridesmaid'. New adaptations of part scenes from 'Peace' by Aristophanes and 'Oliver Twist' by Charles Dickens are also included.

## TOGETHER NOW
### ORIGINAL DUOLOGUES

Ken Pickering
ISBN 0 9537770 1 4

This collection of short duologues includes extracts from Ken Pickering's longer works together with new original pieces. The variety of experiences explored in the scenes can all be easily identified with, such as an awkward situation, 'You Tell Her', and the journey of self knowledge in 'Gilgamesh', whilst 'Mobile phones', 'Sales' and 'Food' observe realistic situations in an interesting and perceptive way. Other duologues based on well known stories include 'Snow White' and 'The Pilgrim's Progress'. Each piece has a brief background description and acting notes. The scenes have syllabus recommendation for a number of examination boards and wide variety of theatrical and school applications.

## MONOLOGUES AND DUOLOGUES

### SHAKESPEARE THE REWRITES

Claire Jones
ISBN 0 9522224 8 5

A collection of short monologues and duologues for female players. The scenes are from rewrites of Shakespeare plays from 1670 to the present day written by authors seeking to embellish original texts for performances, to add prequels or sequels or satisfy their own very personal ideas about production. This material is fresh and unusual and will provide exciting new audition and examination material. Comparisons with the original Shakespeare text are fascinating and this book will provide a useful contribution to Theatre Study work from GCSE to beyond 'A' level. Contributors include James Thurber (Macbeth) Arnold Wesker (Merchant of Venice) and Peter Ustinov (Romanoff and Juliet). The collection also includes a most unusual Japanese version of Hamlet.

## DRAMA LESSONS IN ACTION

Antoinette Line
ISBN 0 9522224 2 6

Resource material suitable for classroom and assembly use for teachers of junior and secondary age pupils. Lessons are taught through improvisation, these are not presented as 'model lessons' but provide ideas for adaptation and further development. Lessons include warm-up and speech exercises and many themes are developed through feelings such as timidity, resentfulness, sensitivity and suspicion. Material can be used by groups of varying sizes and pupils are asked to respond to interesting texts from a diverse selection of well known authors including: Roald Dahl, Ogden Nash, John Betjeman, Ted Hughes, Michael Rosen, and Oscar Wilde.

## AAARGH TO ZIZZ
### 135 DRAMA GAMES

Graeme Talboys
ISBN 0 9537770 5 7

This valuable resource material has been created by a drama teacher and used mostly in formal drama lessons but also in informal situations such as clubs and parties. The games are extremely flexible, from warm up to cool down, inspiration to conclusion and from deadly serious to purest fun and the wide variety ranges from laughing and rhythm activities to building a sentence and word association. Games such as Do You Like Your Neighbour? could be used as part of a PSHE programme together with many of the activities connected with 'fair play'. The games are easily adapted and each has notes on setting up details of straightforward resources needed. All this material has been used with a wide range of young people in the 10 - 18 year age range.

## DRAMA•DANCE•SINGING
### TEACHER RESOURCE BOOK

edited by John Nicholas
ISBN 0 9537770 2 2

This collection of drama, dance and singing lesson activities has been drawn from a bank of ideas used by the Stagecoach Theatre Arts Schools teachers. Clearly presented lessons include speech and drama exercises, games and improvisations often developed as a response to emotions. Dance activities include warm-ups, basic dance positions, improvisations, versatile dance exercises and routines while singing activities help to develop rhythm and notation as well as providing enjoyable games to develop the voice. Activities can be easily adapted for large or small group use and are suitable for 6 - 16 year olds in a fun yet challenging way.

## MUSICAL PLAYS

### THREE CHEERS FOR MRS BUTLER   adapted by Vicky Ireland
ISBN 0 9537770 4 9

This versatile musical play about everyday school life is for anyone who has ever been to school. It features the poems and characters created by Allan Ahlberg with a foreword by Michael Rosen, songs by Colin Matthews and Steven Markwick and was first performed at the Polka Theatre for Children, London. The two acts of 40 minutes each can be performed by children, adults or a mixture of both and the play can be produced with a minimum cast of 7 or a large cast of any size, with or without music and songs, as well as having a wide variety of other musical and dramatic applications.

### INTRODUCING OSCAR                 Veronica Bennetts
The Selfish Giant & The Happy Prince     ISBN 0 9537770 3 0

Oscar Wilde's timeless stories for children have been chosen for adaptation because of the rich opportunities offered for imaginative exploration and the capacity to vividly illuminate many aspects of the human condition. The original dialogue, lyrics and music by Veronica Bennetts can be adapted and modified according to the needs of the pupils and individual schools or drama groups. The Selfish Giant runs for 25 minutes and The Happy Prince for 1 hour 15 minutes. Both musical can be used for Trinity College, *London.* examinations and are ideal for end of term productions, for drama groups and primary and secondary schools.

## TEENAGE PLAYS

### WHAT IS THE MATTER WITH MARY JANE?   Wendy Harmer
ISBN 0 9522224 4 2

This monodrama about a recovering anorexic and bulimic takes the audience into the painful reality of a young woman afflicted by eating disorders. The play is based on the personal experience of actress Sancia Robinson and has proved hugely popular in Australia. It is written with warmth and extraordinary honesty and the language, humour and style appeal to current youth culture. A study guide for teachers and students by Dianne Mackenzie, Curriculum Officer for English and Drama, New South Wales is included in this English edition ensuring that the material is ideal for use in the secondary school classroom and for PSHE studies, drama departments in schools and colleges in addition to amateur and professional performance.

## X-STACY

**Margery Forde**
**ISBN 0 9522224 9 3**

Margery Forde's powerful play centres on the rave culture and illicit teenage drug use and asks tough questions about family, friends and mutual responsibilities. The play has proved hugely successful in Australia and this English edition is published with extensive teachers' notes by Helen Radian, Lecturer of Drama at Queensland University of Technology, to enrich its value for the secondary school classroom, PSHE studies, English and drama departments.

*ONE ACT PLAYS*

## SUGAR ON SUNDAYS
AND OTHER PLAYS

**Andrew Gordon**
**ISBN 0 9522224 3 4**

A collection of six one act plays bringing history alive through drama. History is viewed through the eyes of ordinary people and each play is packed with details about everyday life, important events and developments of the period. The plays can be used as classroom drama, for school performances and group acting examinations and also as shared texts for the literacy hour. The plays are suitable for children from Key Stage 2 upwards and are 40-50 minutes in length and explore Ancient Egypt, Ancient Greece, Anglo-Saxon and Viking Times, Victorian Britain and the Second World War. A glossary of key words helps to develop children's historical understanding of National Curriculum History Topics and the plays provide opportunities for children to enjoy role play and performance.

*TEENAGE SCENES*

## JELLY BEANS

**Joseph McNair Stover**
**ISBN 0 9522224 7 7**

The distinctive style and deceptively simple logic of American writer Joseph McNair Stover has universal appeal with scenes that vary in tone from whimsical to serious and focus on young peoples relationships in the contemporary world. The 10 to 15 minute original scenes for 2,3, and 4 players are suitable for 11 year old students through to adult. Minimal use of sets and props makes Jelly Beans ideal for group acting examinations, classroom drama, assemblies, and a wide variety of additional theatrical applications.